Produced & Published

by

CREDITS

Research, Composition & Text	James A. Bates, Danielle Aphessetche, Charles Stalter
Sculpture (Contributing Artist)	P. Apsit
Artwork (Contributing Artist)	Ed Arambula, Pete McCabe
Photography & Printing	Sammy Lee
Original Designs (Copyrighted)	Max E. Duncan

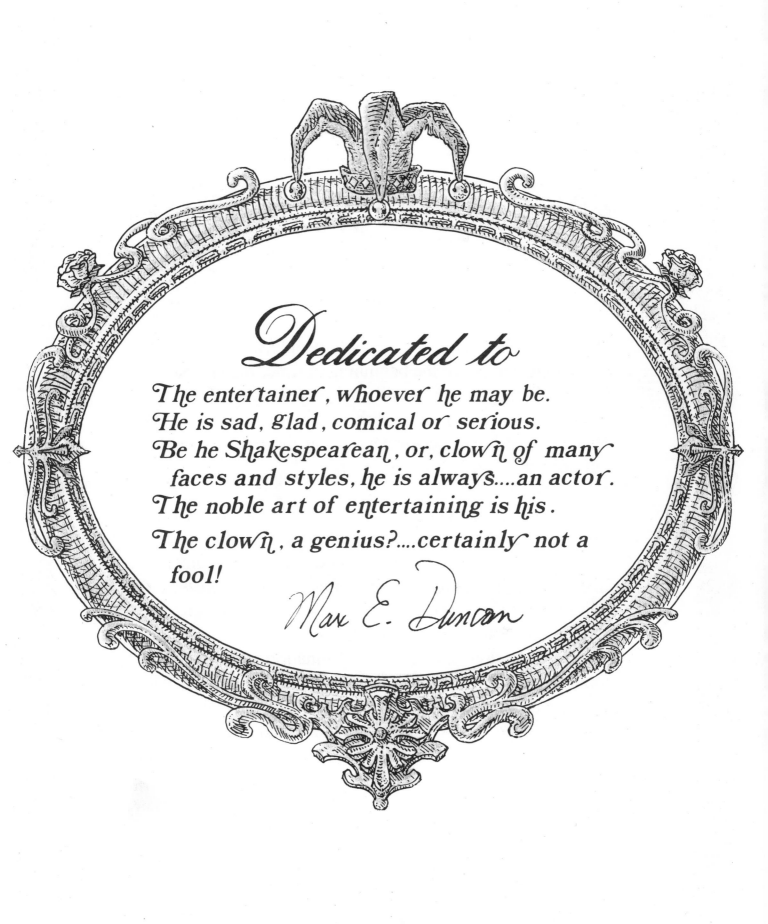

Dedicated to

The entertainer, whoever he may be.
He is sad, glad, comical or serious.
Be he Shakespearean, or, clown of many
    faces and styles, he is always....an actor.
The noble art of entertaining is his.
The clown, a genius?....certainly not a
    fool!

Max E. Duncan

INTRODUCTION

This treatise is a salute to the noble people who give us the gift of laughter. Since the beginning of time, man has found the absurd, the ridiculous and unexpected a source and tool of amusement. The masters of these tools have evolved from early Greco-Roman performers to the modern day clowns and comics.

It has been said "laughter is close to tears" and indeed, often the response to our world's pains has been a new form of comedy. The history of clowns and comedic entertainers is an evolution that spans the world. Each nation expressed its own reaction to war, peace, prosperity and poverty, creating a cross breeding of ideas, rhetoric and costume. The age of communication enhanced this pollination and clowns and comedic entertainers around the world became familiar with their peers, inspiring new growth and diversity of performance. Many clowns and comedic entertainers became famous and personalities emerged as leading innovators in their field.

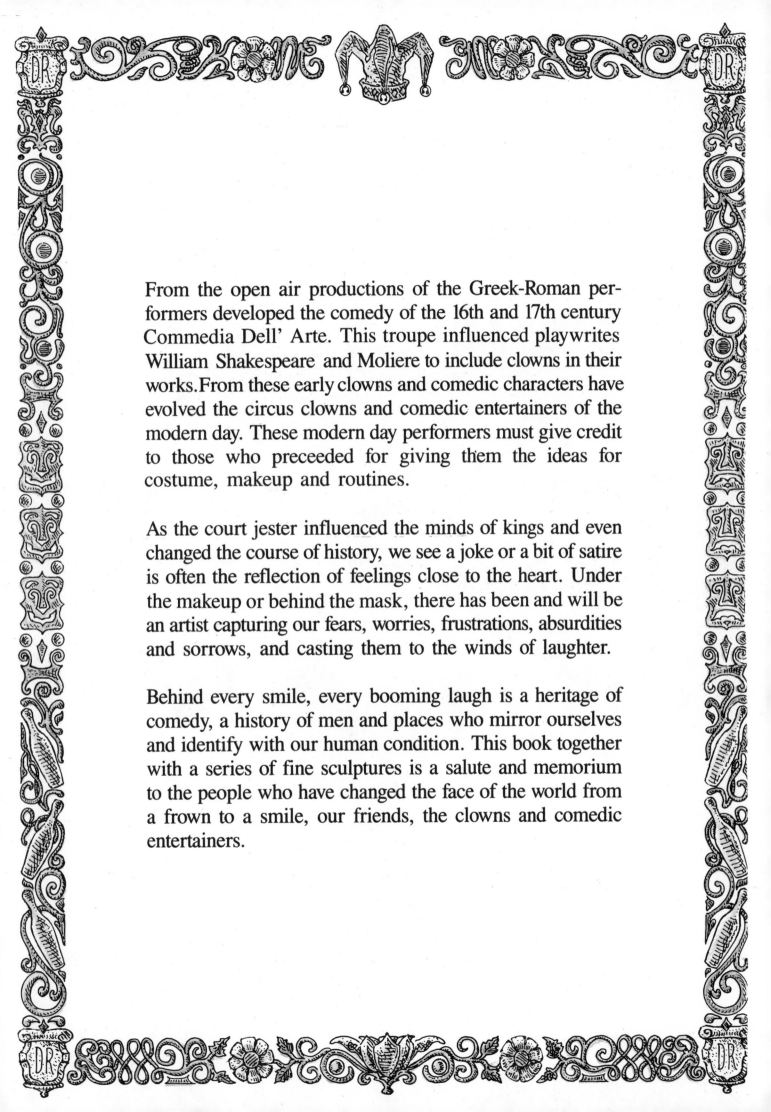

From the open air productions of the Greek-Roman performers developed the comedy of the 16th and 17th century Commedia Dell' Arte. This troupe influenced playwrites William Shakespeare and Moliere to include clowns in their works. From these early clowns and comedic characters have evolved the circus clowns and comedic entertainers of the modern day. These modern day performers must give credit to those who preceeded for giving them the ideas for costume, makeup and routines.

As the court jester influenced the minds of kings and even changed the course of history, we see a joke or a bit of satire is often the reflection of feelings close to the heart. Under the makeup or behind the mask, there has been and will be an artist capturing our fears, worries, frustrations, absurdities and sorrows, and casting them to the winds of laughter.

Behind every smile, every booming laugh is a heritage of comedy, a history of men and places who mirror ourselves and identify with our human condition. This book together with a series of fine sculptures is a salute and memorium to the people who have changed the face of the world from a frown to a smile, our friends, the clowns and comedic entertainers.

THE GRECO ~ ROMAN

Born in the early days of theatre, the art of clowning began with pantomime.

Originating with the Romans, pantomime was a means of projecting an actors part to the back rows of the arena. The lively, exaggerated movement thrilled audiences. The new phenomenon was soon taken to Greece where it replaced the comedies of Menander and Aristophanes. Actors pressed further into the new expression exploring a release of energy and comedic form unfettered by traditional theatre.

Out of this era of creative thinking the mask was introduced. The exaggerated smiles and frowns portrayed in face size carvings of wood and Papier-Mâché were visible to audiences seated too far away to see the faces of the actors. The idea of changing the face with masks and elaborate paint took hold. The clown and his tradition began to carve a permanent place in theatre.

From this humble beginning we start the story of our richest comedy brought to us by our fanciful friend, the clown.

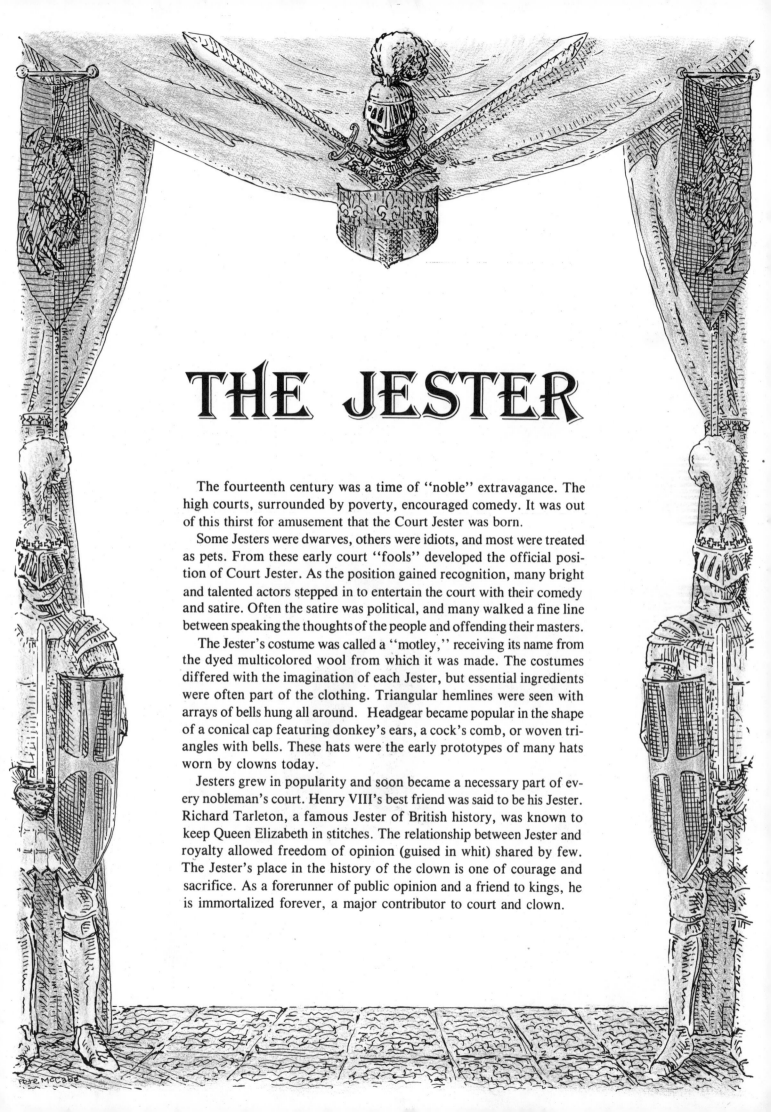

THE JESTER

The fourteenth century was a time of "noble" extravagance. The high courts, surrounded by poverty, encouraged comedy. It was out of this thirst for amusement that the Court Jester was born.

Some Jesters were dwarves, others were idiots, and most were treated as pets. From these early court "fools" developed the official position of Court Jester. As the position gained recognition, many bright and talented actors stepped in to entertain the court with their comedy and satire. Often the satire was political, and many walked a fine line between speaking the thoughts of the people and offending their masters.

The Jester's costume was called a "motley," receiving its name from the dyed multicolored wool from which it was made. The costumes differed with the imagination of each Jester, but essential ingredients were often part of the clothing. Triangular hemlines were seen with arrays of bells hung all around. Headgear became popular in the shape of a conical cap featuring donkey's ears, a cock's comb, or woven triangles with bells. These hats were the early prototypes of many hats worn by clowns today.

Jesters grew in popularity and soon became a necessary part of every nobleman's court. Henry VIII's best friend was said to be his Jester. Richard Tarleton, a famous Jester of British history, was known to keep Queen Elizabeth in stitches. The relationship between Jester and royalty allowed freedom of opinion (guised in whit) shared by few. The Jester's place in the history of the clown is one of courage and sacrifice. As a forerunner of public opinion and a friend to kings, he is immortalized forever, a major contributor to court and clown.

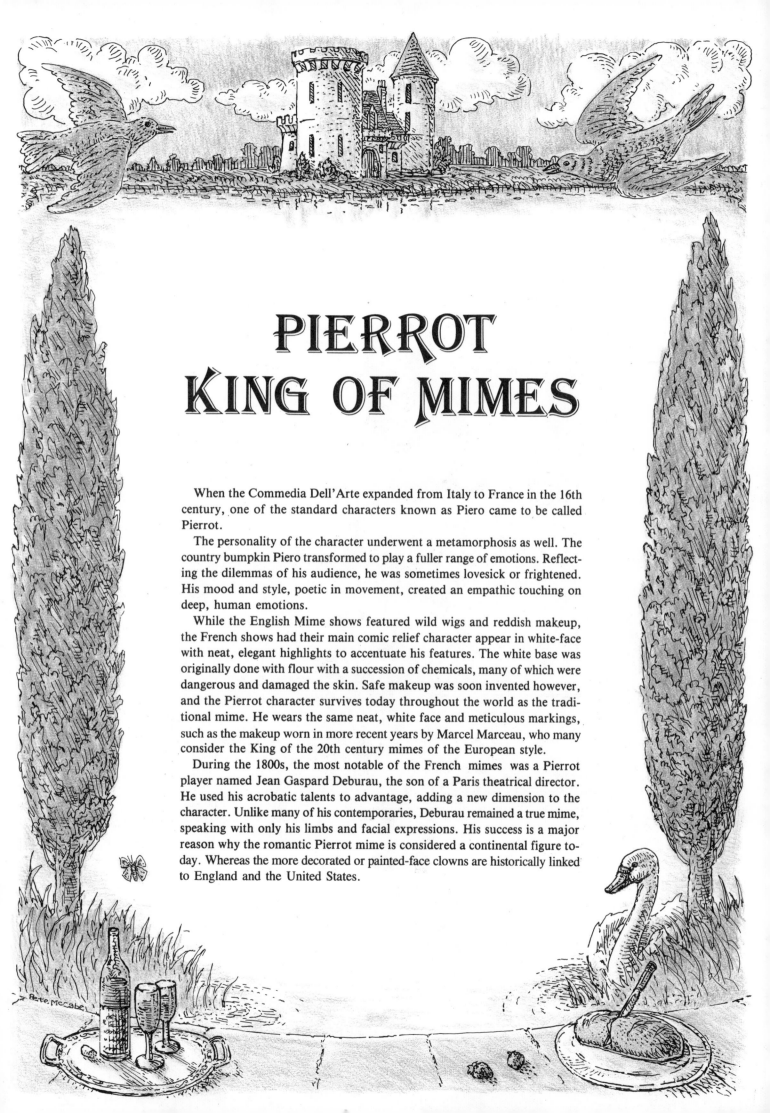

PIERROT
KING OF MIMES

When the Commedia Dell'Arte expanded from Italy to France in the 16th century, one of the standard characters known as Piero came to be called Pierrot.

The personality of the character underwent a metamorphosis as well. The country bumpkin Piero transformed to play a fuller range of emotions. Reflecting the dilemmas of his audience, he was sometimes lovesick or frightened. His mood and style, poetic in movement, created an empathic touching on deep, human emotions.

While the English Mime shows featured wild wigs and reddish makeup, the French shows had their main comic relief character appear in white-face with neat, elegant highlights to accentuate his features. The white base was originally done with flour with a succession of chemicals, many of which were dangerous and damaged the skin. Safe makeup was soon invented however, and the Pierrot character survives today throughout the world as the traditional mime. He wears the same neat, white face and meticulous markings, such as the makeup worn in more recent years by Marcel Marceau, who many consider the King of the 20th century mimes of the European style.

During the 1800s, the most notable of the French mimes was a Pierrot player named Jean Gaspard Deburau, the son of a Paris theatrical director. He used his acrobatic talents to advantage, adding a new dimension to the character. Unlike many of his contemporaries, Deburau remained a true mime, speaking with only his limbs and facial expressions. His success is a major reason why the romantic Pierrot mime is considered a continental figure today. Whereas the more decorated or painted-face clowns are historically linked to England and the United States.

HARLEQUIN

HARLEQUIN

The evolution of clowning reached professional status by the 16th century. Actors devoted their careers to clowning and the Commedia Dell' Arte formed as the first professional touring company in Italy. The public responded with enthusiasm and the troupe played to full houses.

Certain character roles developed and the audiences came to expect appearances by them in each performance. Their costumes and dialects also became stylized to the point where audiences instantly knew who each character was by his costume.

The chief character was "Arlecchino", a masked figure who engaged in many slapstick routines. Arlecchino was later changed to Harlequin when the Commedia Dell' Arte finally arrived in England.

The first of the Harlequins were characterized as simpletons, but they evolved into a more cunning character...ones who would use their presumed absence of intelligence to trick the unwary.

The Harlequin character was noted for his knockabout, slapstick scenes, often tripping over his own feet, knocking over scenery, and sometimes even taking his shenanigans into the audience.

Though some of the other characters were more clownlike than the Harlequin, it is he who often receives the credit as the forerunner of today's classical clown.

Pete McCabe

GROTESQUE

In France between 1800 and 1850, a new image was developing. The French Grotesque began to emerge as a character not only expert in costume and acting, but also as an acrobat. His skills involved horses, rope walking, tumbling and balancing, all embellished with comic improvisation.

The first Grotesque artist was Jean Gontard, celebrated as the buffoon of Astley's, a famous night spot in Paris. Later, his popularity was overshadowed by the most popular Grotesque of the era, Jean-Batiste Auriol, whose performances were described as "encyclopedic". Auriol was a juggler, tumbler, rope dancer, and equestrian as well as comedian. Because of his remarkable feats of acrobatics one circus historian credits him with equal importance to the equestrian, then the most important of the circus performers.

This idea of clowning and performing acrobatics was a great step towards our modern circus performances. The history of daring men in costume is now our most extravagant colorful touring show under the "Big Top".

PANTALONE

With a hooked nose and an almost witch-like appearance, Pantalone embodied the spirit of meddlesome evil in the plays of the Commedia Dell' Arte.

Pantalone's actions were not as sinister as his costume. He simply meddled in the affairs of others, primarily those of Arlecchino and the maid Colombine, the female character Arlecchino was usually courting.

The old codger would always try to thwart the romance, a precursor to the eventual plot of Romeo and Juliet. Love would eventually triumph to the immediate chagrin and eventual acceptance of the old meddler.

The foregoing was by no means a script that was unfailingly adhered to in the harlequinade. Pantalone, as would the other characters, become involved in a series of wild scenes which differed from show to show. However, the eventual result was usually the same. Harlequin would win, Pantalone would lose.

In many ways, Pantalone was the first classical melodramatic villain. His character finds a place in clowning with a sneer, our favorite antagonist deserving boo's and perhaps a timely tomato.

PULCINELLA

With a trip and pratfall, Pulcinella rose to fame flying his banner of foolery in the guise of a smiling idiot with a fat stomach. His fellow players of the Commedia Dell' Arte found his inability to perform the simplest of tasks a source of constant entertainment. The audience loved his clumsy attempts and he soon found a permanent place among his fellow clowns and players as a perfect "butt" of any joke. Pulcinella was greedy and boorish, but used his charm to swindle whomever he could.

Pulcinella, who was later known as "Punch" in England, was the character who made food the classic prop for the clown. Gluttony was transformed from a vice into an art form, with Pulcinella gorging himself with sausages pilfered from the other characters.

Once the character became "Punch" in England, he was so popular that he became immortalized as a puppet, featuring the hooked nose which was part of the costume in the Commedia Dell' Arte but without the mask.

Punch and Judy proceeded to grow in fame. Punch evolved to a clown immortalized by children and their love for his silly puppet scenarios.

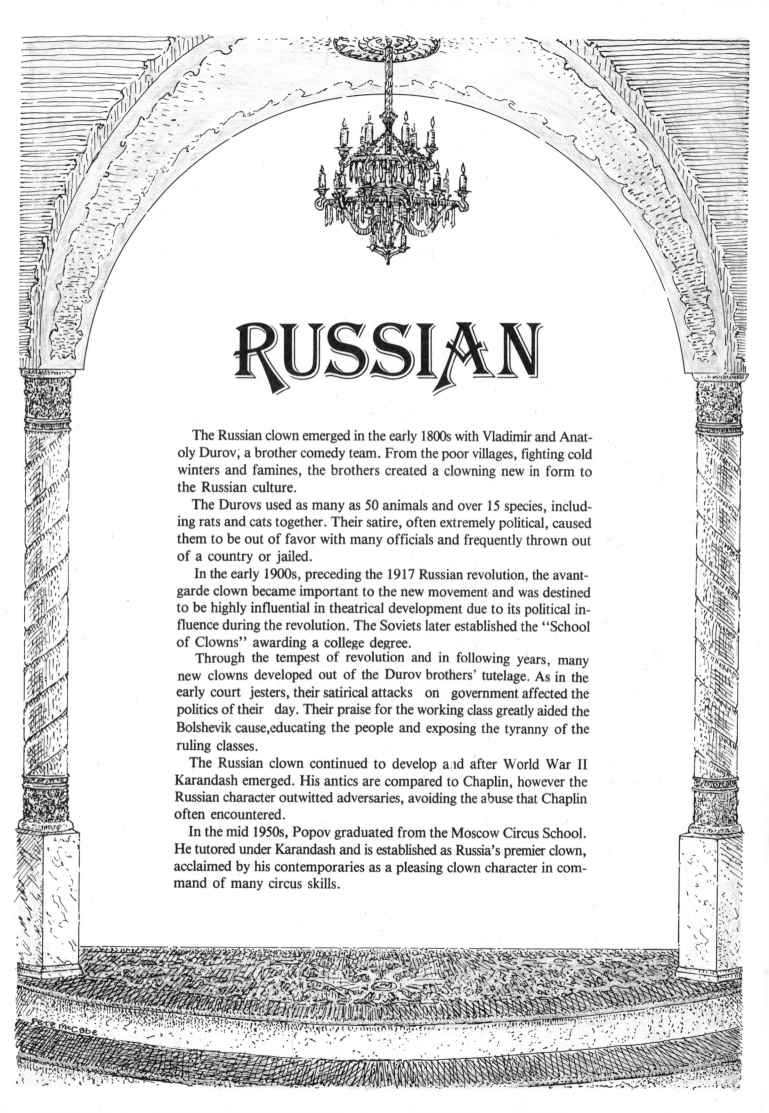

RUSSIAN

The Russian clown emerged in the early 1800s with Vladimir and Anatoly Durov, a brother comedy team. From the poor villages, fighting cold winters and famines, the brothers created a clowning new in form to the Russian culture.

The Durovs used as many as 50 animals and over 15 species, including rats and cats together. Their satire, often extremely political, caused them to be out of favor with many officials and frequently thrown out of a country or jailed.

In the early 1900s, preceding the 1917 Russian revolution, the avantgarde clown became important to the new movement and was destined to be highly influential in theatrical development due to its political influence during the revolution. The Soviets later established the "School of Clowns" awarding a college degree.

Through the tempest of revolution and in following years, many new clowns developed out of the Durov brothers' tutelage. As in the early court jesters, their satirical attacks on government affected the politics of their day. Their praise for the working class greatly aided the Bolshevik cause, educating the people and exposing the tyranny of the ruling classes.

The Russian clown continued to develop and after World War II Karandash emerged. His antics are compared to Chaplin, however the Russian character outwitted adversaries, avoiding the abuse that Chaplin often encountered.

In the mid 1950s, Popov graduated from the Moscow Circus School. He tutored under Karandash and is established as Russia's premier clown, acclaimed by his contemporaries as a pleasing clown character in command of many circus skills.

Pete McCabe

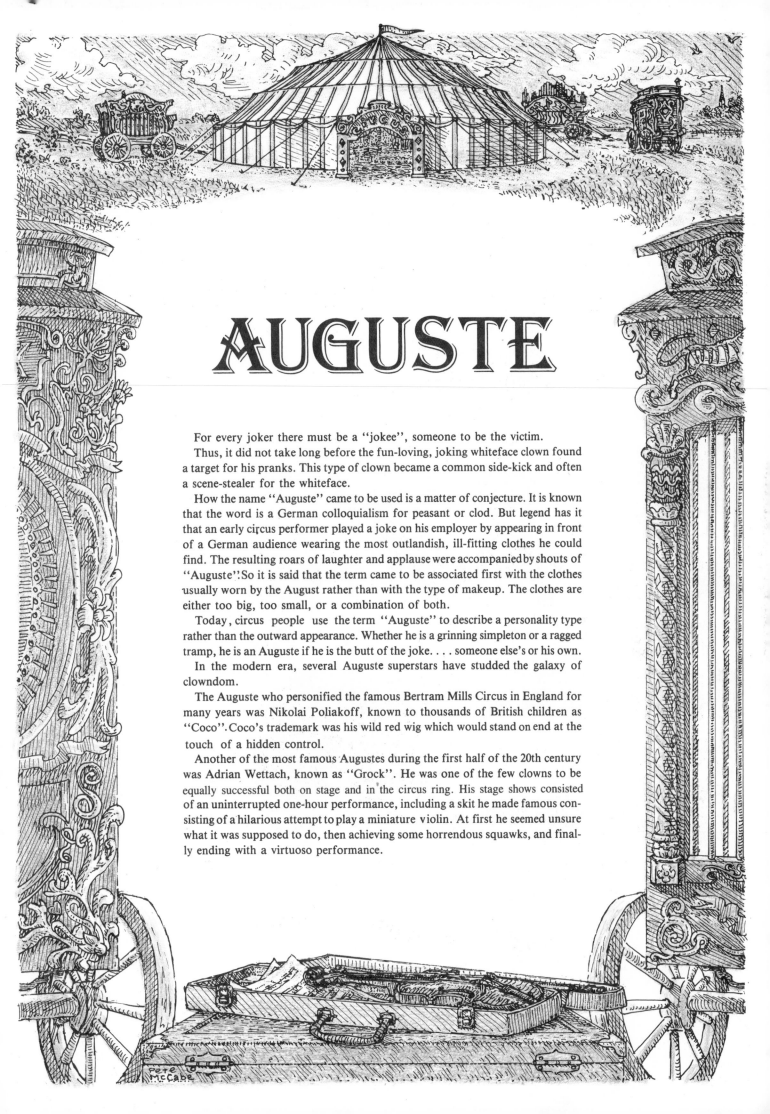

AUGUSTE

For every joker there must be a "jokee", someone to be the victim.

Thus, it did not take long before the fun-loving, joking whiteface clown found a target for his pranks. This type of clown became a common side-kick and often a scene-stealer for the whiteface.

How the name "Auguste" came to be used is a matter of conjecture. It is known that the word is a German colloquialism for peasant or clod. But legend has it that an early circus performer played a joke on his employer by appearing in front of a German audience wearing the most outlandish, ill-fitting clothes he could find. The resulting roars of laughter and applause were accompanied by shouts of "Auguste". So it is said that the term came to be associated first with the clothes usually worn by the August rather than with the type of makeup. The clothes are either too big, too small, or a combination of both.

Today, circus people use the term "Auguste" to describe a personality type rather than the outward appearance. Whether he is a grinning simpleton or a ragged tramp, he is an Auguste if he is the butt of the joke. . . . someone else's or his own.

In the modern era, several Auguste superstars have studded the galaxy of clowndom.

The Auguste who personified the famous Bertram Mills Circus in England for many years was Nikolai Poliakoff, known to thousands of British children as "Coco". Coco's trademark was his wild red wig which would stand on end at the touch of a hidden control.

Another of the most famous Augustes during the first half of the 20th century was Adrian Wettach, known as "Grock". He was one of the few clowns to be equally successful both on stage and in the circus ring. His stage shows consisted of an uninterrupted one-hour performance, including a skit he made famous consisting of a hilarious attempt to play a miniature violin. At first he seemed unsure what it was supposed to do, then achieving some horrendous squawks, and finally ending with a virtuoso performance.

SLAPSTICK

By the latter part of the 18th Century, the highest form of entertainment in England was the mime show. The English acceptance of the character, Harlequin, had transformed the Italian-French Commedia Dell' Arte into a show with a decidedly English flavor.

The "dumb show" had gradually introduced comic relief parts, bit-players wearing red wigs and blotches of red makeup. They played the role of the country yokel and took pratfalls on stage followed by roars of laughter from the audience. Due to audience demand, these minor players in the world of mime soon had the lead role. The clown had arrived.

It was at this time that the man whose name became synonymous with the word "clown" got his start. His name was Joseph Grimaldi.

During Grimaldi's career he revolutionized the art of makeup. He exaggerated the country yokel look by using the white-face makeup of the more serious French mime, and added hilarious markings to highlight his features. He topped it off with bright tufts of hair on a bald head. This look became the standard for whiteface clowns to this day.

Joseph Grimaldi became the most important figure in the history of clowns. For generations clowns have called themselves "Joey". What greater tribute can a person have from his peers. It was a wonderful achievement for a clown who never appeared in a circus.

UNCLE SAM

Uncle Sam, our greatest patriot, was born as a clown amidst early America's reaching for its own personal statement of comedic expression. Most of the Uncle Sam clowns are on stilts, possibly a patriotic message that America stands tall.

In a world where art imitates life, one would think that an anonymous clown once decided to dress like Uncle Sam for his performance. Actually, the opposite is true. Life imitated art.

Dan Rice, an American circus strongman-turned clown, developed a novel costume in the 1840s. He used no makeup, but he wore a unique outfit consisting of striped suit and beard. With an unusual act, including readings of Shakespeare in backwoods dialect, he became famous throughout the country and billed himself as "America's Favorite Clown". Rice became a sought-after speaker and even ran for Congress. President Lincoln, needing a morale-builder during the dark times of the Civil War, used Rice's image as the basis for Uncle Sam.

Uncle Sam went on to become a lasting statement of American values. He has promoted drafts, war bonds, and peacetime projects. His face is the immortal visage of American democracy calling us all to remember our heritage and responsibilities as Americans.

E PLURIBUS UNUM

Pete McCabe

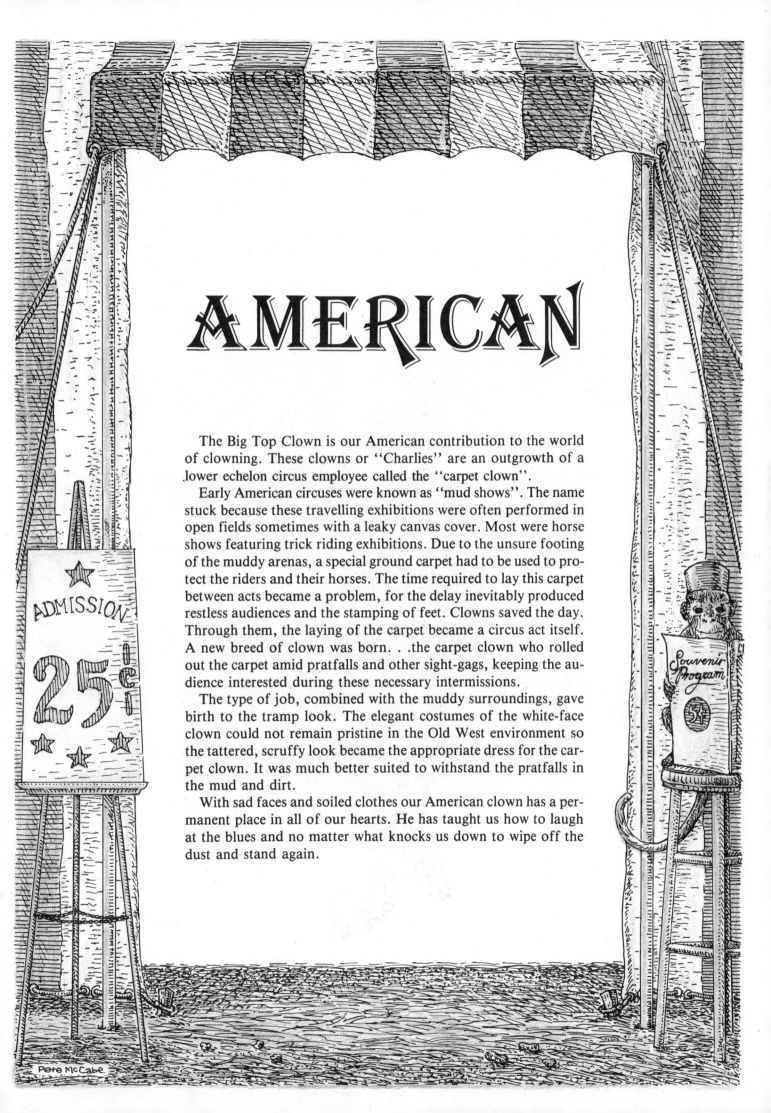

AMERICAN

The Big Top Clown is our American contribution to the world of clowning. These clowns or "Charlies" are an outgrowth of a lower echelon circus employee called the "carpet clown".

Early American circuses were known as "mud shows". The name stuck because these travelling exhibitions were often performed in open fields sometimes with a leaky canvas cover. Most were horse shows featuring trick riding exhibitions. Due to the unsure footing of the muddy arenas, a special ground carpet had to be used to protect the riders and their horses. The time required to lay this carpet between acts became a problem, for the delay inevitably produced restless audiences and the stamping of feet. Clowns saved the day. Through them, the laying of the carpet became a circus act itself. A new breed of clown was born. . .the carpet clown who rolled out the carpet amid pratfalls and other sight-gags, keeping the audience interested during these necessary intermissions.

The type of job, combined with the muddy surroundings, gave birth to the tramp look. The elegant costumes of the white-face clown could not remain pristine in the Old West environment so the tattered, scruffy look became the appropriate dress for the carpet clown. It was much better suited to withstand the pratfalls in the mud and dirt.

With sad faces and soiled clothes our American clown has a permanent place in all of our hearts. He has taught us how to laugh at the blues and no matter what knocks us down to wipe off the dust and stand again.

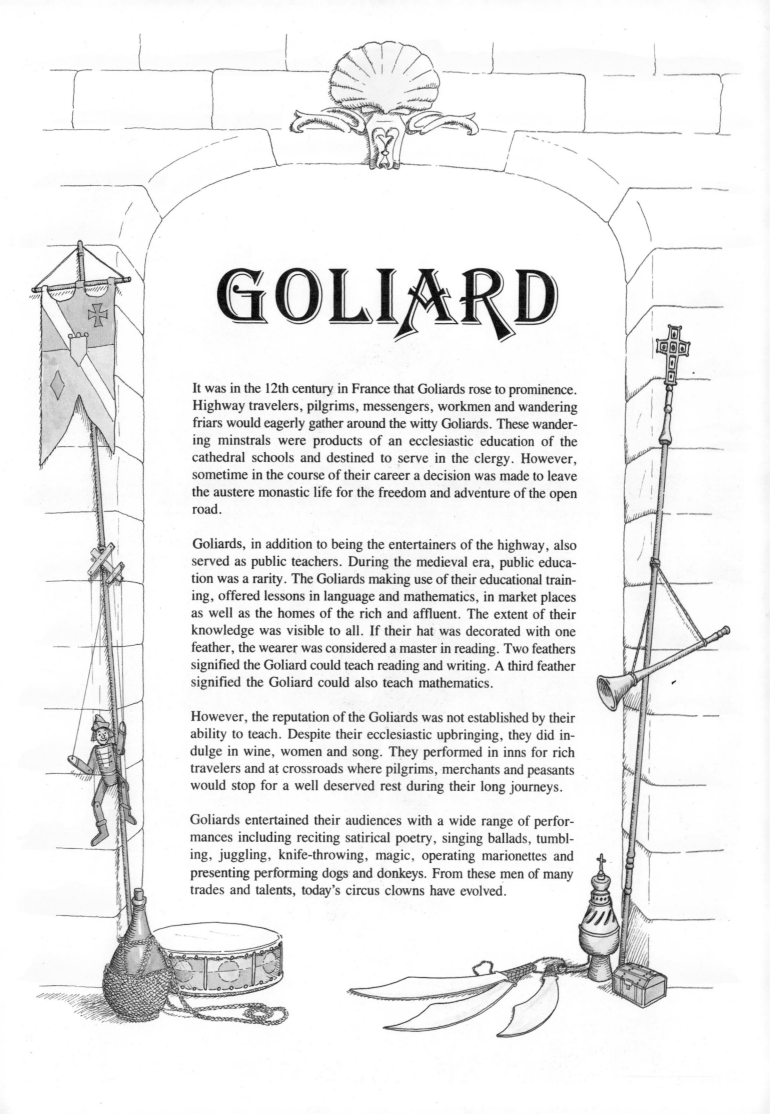

GOLIARD

It was in the 12th century in France that Goliards rose to prominence. Highway travelers, pilgrims, messengers, workmen and wandering friars would eagerly gather around the witty Goliards. These wandering minstrals were products of an ecclesiastic education of the cathedral schools and destined to serve in the clergy. However, sometime in the course of their career a decision was made to leave the austere monastic life for the freedom and adventure of the open road.

Goliards, in addition to being the entertainers of the highway, also served as public teachers. During the medieval era, public education was a rarity. The Goliards making use of their educational training, offered lessons in language and mathematics, in market places as well as the homes of the rich and affluent. The extent of their knowledge was visible to all. If their hat was decorated with one feather, the wearer was considered a master in reading. Two feathers signified the Goliard could teach reading and writing. A third feather signified the Goliard could also teach mathematics.

However, the reputation of the Goliards was not established by their ability to teach. Despite their ecclesiastic upbringing, they did indulge in wine, women and song. They performed in inns for rich travelers and at crossroads where pilgrims, merchants and peasants would stop for a well deserved rest during their long journeys.

Goliards entertained their audiences with a wide range of performances including reciting satirical poetry, singing ballads, tumbling, juggling, knife-throwing, magic, operating marionettes and presenting performing dogs and donkeys. From these men of many trades and talents, today's circus clowns have evolved.

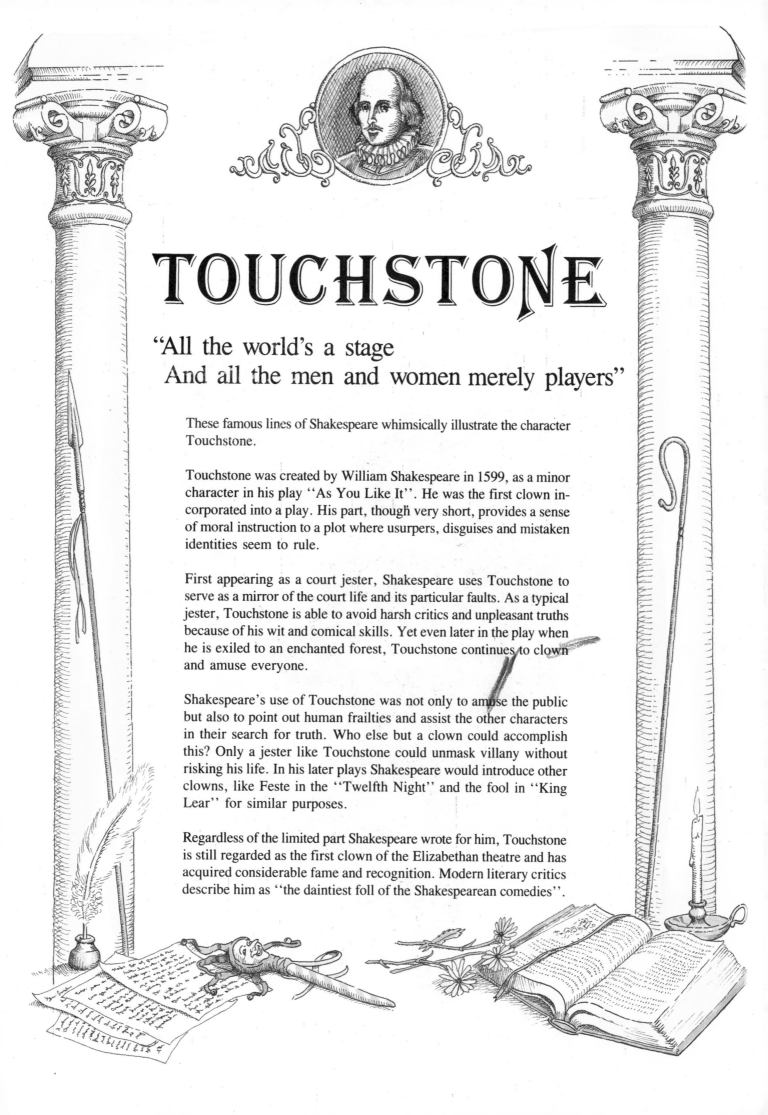

TOUCHSTONE

"All the world's a stage
And all the men and women merely players"

These famous lines of Shakespeare whimsically illustrate the character Touchstone.

Touchstone was created by William Shakespeare in 1599, as a minor character in his play "As You Like It". He was the first clown incorporated into a play. His part, though very short, provides a sense of moral instruction to a plot where usurpers, disguises and mistaken identities seem to rule.

First appearing as a court jester, Shakespeare uses Touchstone to serve as a mirror of the court life and its particular faults. As a typical jester, Touchstone is able to avoid harsh critics and unpleasant truths because of his wit and comical skills. Yet even later in the play when he is exiled to an enchanted forest, Touchstone continues to clown and amuse everyone.

Shakespeare's use of Touchstone was not only to amuse the public but also to point out human frailties and assist the other characters in their search for truth. Who else but a clown could accomplish this? Only a jester like Touchstone could unmask villany without risking his life. In his later plays Shakespeare would introduce other clowns, like Feste in the "Twelfth Night" and the fool in "King Lear" for similar purposes.

Regardless of the limited part Shakespeare wrote for him, Touchstone is still regarded as the first clown of the Elizabethan theatre and has acquired considerable fame and recognition. Modern literary critics describe him as "the daintiest foll of the Shakespearean comedies".

FESTE

The character of Feste was first introduced in 1601 in the play the "Twelfth Night" by William Shakespeare. Feste is a jester in the court of the Duke of Illarya, and much like the character Touchstone, uses his wit to bring coherence and a happy ending to the play.

The "Twelfth Night" is one of the most profound of the Shakespearean golden comedies. It was commissioned by a group of young lawyers and conceived as a kind of bagatelle. This play was to be performed at a Christmas celebration being held by the lawyers.

The role of Feste was created for Robert Armin, the famous clown of the Shakespearean Company, who was also an excellant writer and musician. Shakespeare created the role of Feste around the musical talents of Armin and incorporated songs and melodies in his play.

Feste plays a key role in the "Twelfth Night". Shakespeare shows that the role of Feste and that of any "fool" or "jester" in general, required great intelligence to act. The "Fool" or "jester" had to have a mature sensitivity to deal with the varying temperments and moods of the superiors, while trying to soothe and entertain them. Throughout the "Twelfth Night", Shakespeare portrays the clown Feste as being clear eyed and wise enough to stand above the others and comment on their follies. Feste alone is immune to the craziness of Illyria, but must hide his wisdom behind verses of a song and funny replies. In a world where everyone is slightly mad, his motley is a badge of knowledge.

"Playing the fool is a wise man art."

TARTAGLIA

In the 16th century, small theatrical companies formed and travelled throughout Italy, performing improvised comedies. They called themselves "Dell' Arte", which means "skilled" as contrasted to the amateurish troupes performing in the royal courts and in universities.

Many of the modern clowns have evolved from the characters who perfomed on the temporary stages of Commedia Dell' Arte. Through many performances, before very diversified audiences, these characters had the opportunity to shape and develop their roles.

One of the characters of the Commedia Dell' Arte, Tartaglia (also known as the Doctor of Law or Balanzoni) played the role of the antagonist to such other characters as Harlequin, Pierrot, Zanni and Colombine. Much like these other characters, Tartaglia's costume was an integral part of his persona. He always appears in dark, gloomy clothes, which were associated with clerical attire. With his long, beaked mask and extravagant manners, Tartaglia became the symbol of hypocrisy. He was also the master of defamation, always eavesdropping and spreading rumors.

The character of Tartaglia was incorporated into French plays in the 17th century. Moliere, the famous French comedy playwrite, included Tartaglia in his satirical comedies. His character "Tartuffe" is a pompous doctor, hypocritical and greedy, a direct portrayal of the character Tartaglia from the Commedia Dell' Arte.

In the 18th century Tartaglia becomes immortalized through the role of Bazile in a Beaumarchais play, which becomes the basis for the Rossini opera "The Barber Seville". This success in opera did not prevent the character Tartaglia from continuing to entertain the popular masses. Tartaglia continued to be seen in the 19th century in melodramas played on shakey stages in small suburbs throughout Europe. Still wearing an oversized dark coat and hiding his face, he was hissed and booed by audiences.

Tartaglia is still the sly, treacherous character who delights the public. Under his less than lovable manners, Tartaglia mirrors a dark side of human nature and allows us to laugh about it.

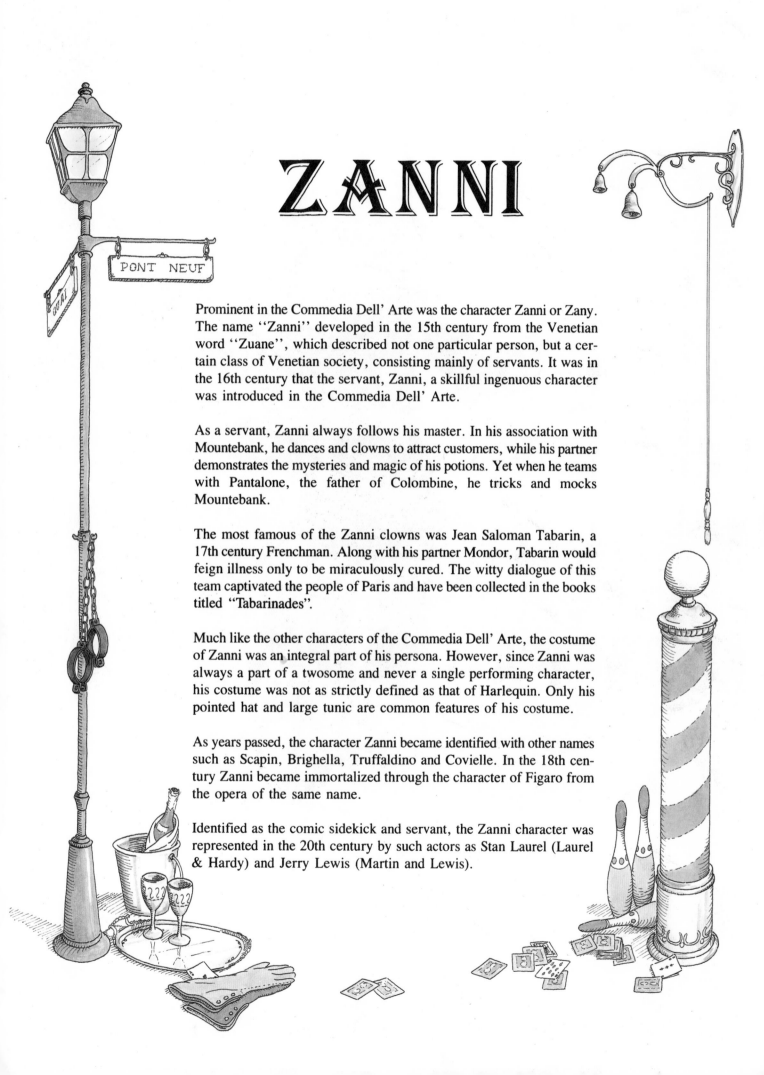

ZANNI

Prominent in the Commedia Dell' Arte was the character Zanni or Zany. The name "Zanni" developed in the 15th century from the Venetian word "Zuane", which described not one particular person, but a certain class of Venetian society, consisting mainly of servants. It was in the 16th century that the servant, Zanni, a skillful ingenuous character was introduced in the Commedia Dell' Arte.

As a servant, Zanni always follows his master. In his association with Mountebank, he dances and clowns to attract customers, while his partner demonstrates the mysteries and magic of his potions. Yet when he teams with Pantalone, the father of Colombine, he tricks and mocks Mountebank.

The most famous of the Zanni clowns was Jean Saloman Tabarin, a 17th century Frenchman. Along with his partner Mondor, Tabarin would feign illness only to be miraculously cured. The witty dialogue of this team captivated the people of Paris and have been collected in the books titled "Tabarinades".

Much like the other characters of the Commedia Dell' Arte, the costume of Zanni was an integral part of his persona. However, since Zanni was always a part of a twosome and never a single performing character, his costume was not as strictly defined as that of Harlequin. Only his pointed hat and large tunic are common features of his costume.

As years passed, the character Zanni became identified with other names such as Scapin, Brighella, Truffaldino and Covielle. In the 18th century Zanni became immortalized through the character of Figaro from the opera of the same name.

Identified as the comic sidekick and servant, the Zanni character was represented in the 20th century by such actors as Stan Laurel (Laurel & Hardy) and Jerry Lewis (Martin and Lewis).

MOUNTEBANK

The Commedia Dell Arte presented three basic types of characters to their audiences: the lovers, who didn't have to be funny; servants, like Zanni, Pierrot and Harlequin; and the masters. One of the most famous master was Mountebank.

The name "Mountebank" literally means "climbed onto a bench (bank)". This bench later became an improvised stage. From this elevated location, Mountebank the merchant or quack doctor, addresses the passerby, trying to sell his magic potions. He adds to the humor and fun of the show by having a trained monkey serve as his companion.

Mountebank was usually seen working with his servant, Zanni. Zanni would mock his master, tumble and play sick, attracting the attention of the people. Mountebank would then start his sale pitch, using made up foreign words to add to the impressiveness of the presentation.

Performing in Paris in the 17th century was the most famous of Mountebank-Zanni teams, Mondor and Tabarin. Mondor, the Mountebank, would address the audiences with claims of being able to extricate all fevers, chills and other illnesses and go as far as to kill the patient to relieve him of his disorder. The witty dialogues of this team captivated the audiences of Paris and have been collected in books titled "Tabarinades".

Mountebank endorsed very scientific qualifications and made unfounded claims upon his very unwary and gullible audiences. William Shakespeare speaks of Mountebank in these unflattering words:

> "As nimble jugglers deceive the eye Disguised cheaters, prating
> mountebanks And many such libertiness of sin."

The tradition of Mountebank continues and is exemplified by the medicine men of the American west and in today's street peddlers, peddling their miracle cures, herbs and pills.

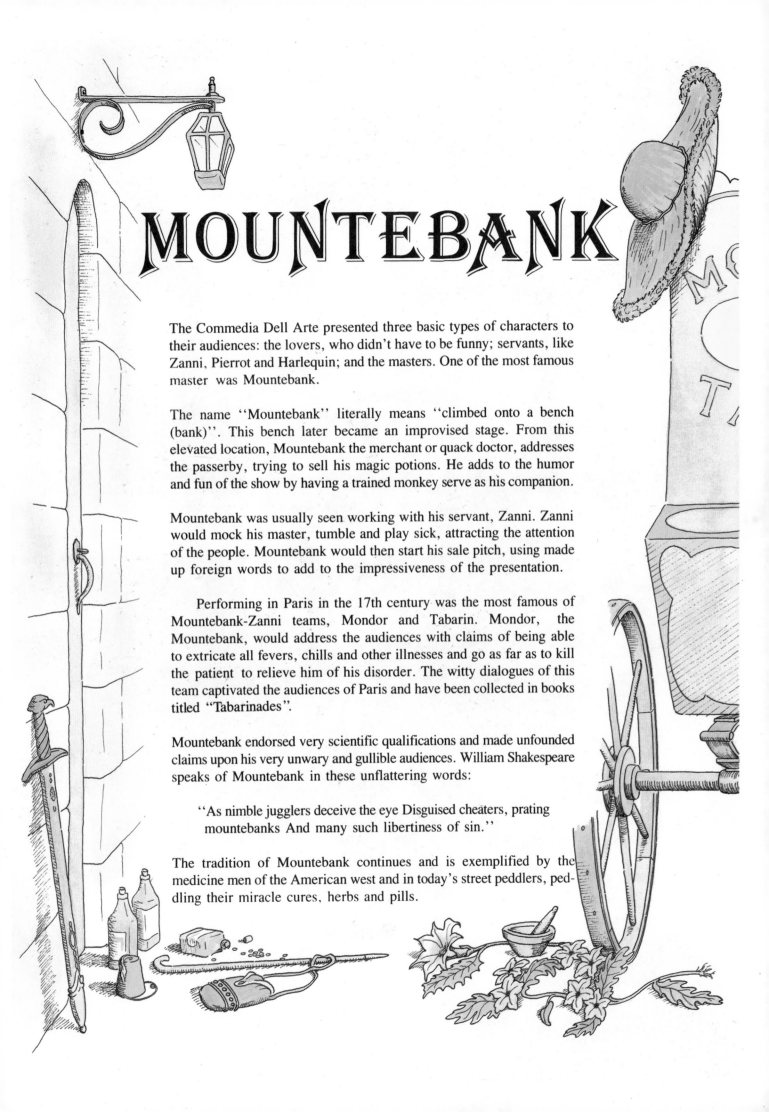

PEDROLINO

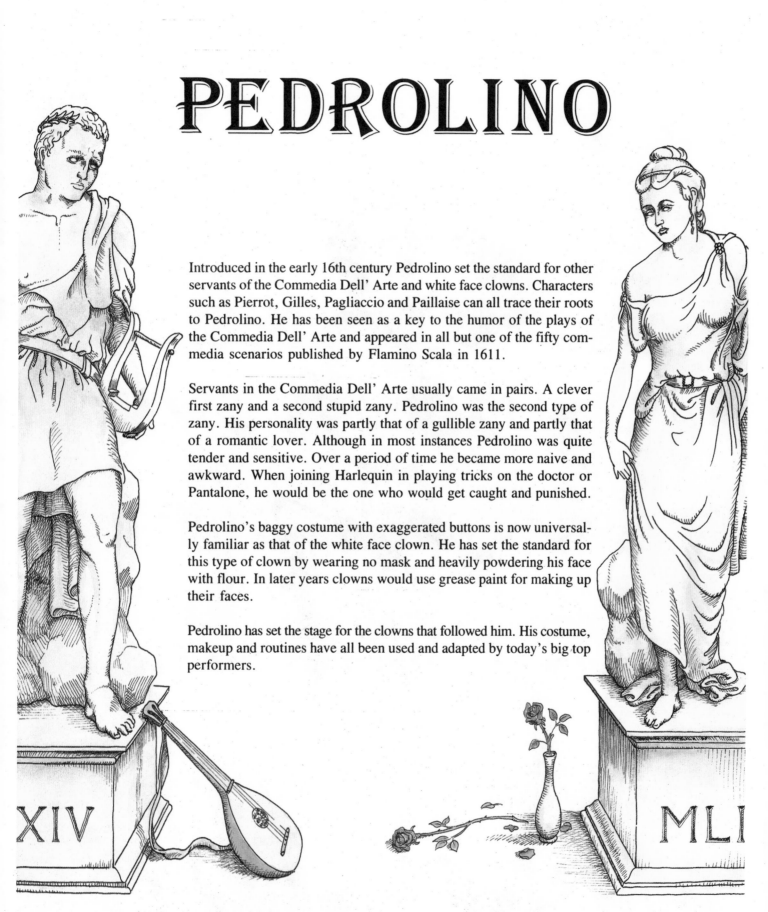

Introduced in the early 16th century Pedrolino set the standard for other servants of the Commedia Dell' Arte and white face clowns. Characters such as Pierrot, Gilles, Pagliaccio and Paillaise can all trace their roots to Pedrolino. He has been seen as a key to the humor of the plays of the Commedia Dell' Arte and appeared in all but one of the fifty commedia scenarios published by Flamino Scala in 1611.

Servants in the Commedia Dell' Arte usually came in pairs. A clever first zany and a second stupid zany. Pedrolino was the second type of zany. His personality was partly that of a gullible zany and partly that of a romantic lover. Although in most instances Pedrolino was quite tender and sensitive. Over a period of time he became more naive and awkward. When joining Harlequin in playing tricks on the doctor or Pantalone, he would be the one who would get caught and punished.

Pedrolino's baggy costume with exaggerated buttons is now universally familiar as that of the white face clown. He has set the standard for this type of clown by wearing no mask and heavily powdering his face with flour. In later years clowns would use grease paint for making up their faces.

Pedrolino has set the stage for the clowns that followed him. His costume, makeup and routines have all been used and adapted by today's big top performers.

THOMASSI

Born in a small village near Venice, Italy in 1683 was one of the most famous Harlequins, Thomassi. Early in his youth Thomassi exhibited an intense fascination for the stage. This fascination led to his joining the Commedia Erudita, a group composed mostly of dilettante amateurs who produced their own literary dramas for the intellectual elite.

It was during this affiliation with the Commedia Erudita that Thomassi started acquiring a knowledge of the acting profession and developing his skills. However, Thomassi soon left the serious theatre of the city for the more exciting life of the popular strolling players of the Commedia Dell' Arte.

With this wandering troupe of actors, Thomassi toured France and Italy. During this time Thomassi established himself in the role of Harlequin. He exhibited trememdous physical skills. Thomassi's favorite and most acclaimed trick involved turning a back somersault, holding a glass of wine, without spilling a drop!

The role of Harlequin, according to actor/author Luigi Riccoboni, was a "continual play of extravagant tricks, violent movements and outrageous rogueries. He was at once insolent, mocking, inept, clownish and emphatically ribald...he was also extraordinarily agile and seemed to be constantly in the air; and I might add that he was a proficient tumbler". This was Thomassi! Drawing from his experience from the Commedia Erudita, Thomassi added a depth of drama to his Harlequin character. He could create laughter or bring tears of sorrow to the eyes of the European audiences, despite the fact that he was wearing the half mask, typical of the servants of the Commedia Dell' Arte.

In less than a half century, Thomassi was able to win the hearts and admiration of audiences in both France and Italy. He developed a style and character that was later copied in the French and English fairground theatres where clowns combined juggling, ropedancing and tumbling in the performances of parades. The tradition of the great Thomassi will never die!

TRAMP

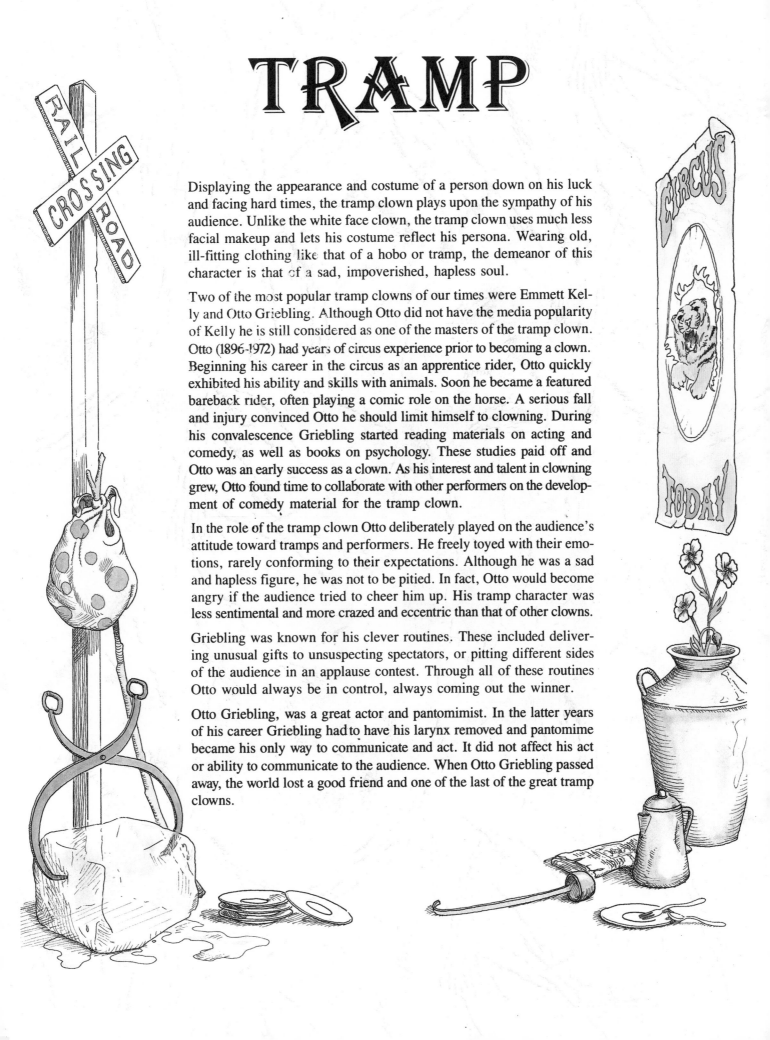

Displaying the appearance and costume of a person down on his luck and facing hard times, the tramp clown plays upon the sympathy of his audience. Unlike the white face clown, the tramp clown uses much less facial makeup and lets his costume reflect his persona. Wearing old, ill-fitting clothing like that of a hobo or tramp, the demeanor of this character is that of a sad, impoverished, hapless soul.

Two of the most popular tramp clowns of our times were Emmett Kelly and Otto Griebling. Although Otto did not have the media popularity of Kelly he is still considered as one of the masters of the tramp clown. Otto (1896-1972) had years of circus experience prior to becoming a clown. Beginning his career in the circus as an apprentice rider, Otto quickly exhibited his ability and skills with animals. Soon he became a featured bareback rider, often playing a comic role on the horse. A serious fall and injury convinced Otto he should limit himself to clowning. During his convalescence Griebling started reading materials on acting and comedy, as well as books on psychology. These studies paid off and Otto was an early success as a clown. As his interest and talent in clowning grew, Otto found time to collaborate with other performers on the development of comedy material for the tramp clown.

In the role of the tramp clown Otto deliberately played on the audience's attitude toward tramps and performers. He freely toyed with their emotions, rarely conforming to their expectations. Although he was a sad and hapless figure, he was not to be pitied. In fact, Otto would become angry if the audience tried to cheer him up. His tramp character was less sentimental and more crazed and eccentric than that of other clowns.

Griebling was known for his clever routines. These included delivering unusual gifts to unsuspecting spectators, or pitting different sides of the audience in an applause contest. Through all of these routines Otto would always be in control, always coming out the winner.

Otto Griebling, was a great actor and pantomimist. In the latter years of his career Griebling had to have his larynx removed and pantomime became his only way to communicate and act. It did not affect his act or ability to communicate to the audience. When Otto Griebling passed away, the world lost a good friend and one of the last of the great tramp clowns.

CIRCUS TONITE

WHITE FACE

From Goliard, Pierrot, Thomassi and other masters of mirth, wit and humor, have evolved the clowns of the 20th century. The clowns we see in today's circuses have developed their acts, skills and persona from these characters. The lessons learned from these early performers have been passed on to the new entertainers of the big top.

This new breed of clowns is represented by three basic types: the white face, tramp and auguste. Following the tradition of such characters as Pedrolino and Pierrot, the white face clown as the name implies, covers his face in white makeup. He then applies additional makeup to create his own special identity. White face clowns have gone as far as to copyright their makeup designs.

White face clowns much like the Goliards, have brought tumbling, juggling and magic into their acts. They strive to keep the audience entertained and in a festive mood through the use of outrageous colored costumes and makeup designs. Their hope is to have people forget their troubles and worries and find a few moments of enjoyment under the big top.

Some of the prominent white face clowns have been Joseph Grimaldi, Lou Jacobs and Chuck Burnes. Burnes followed the traditions that had been learned from his peers and those comedic characters of theatre. Like Goliard, Chuck incorporated magic into his act and always tried to have the audience leave with a smile on their face! Burnes worked many years as a featured clown with Ringling Brothers and Barnum and Bailey circus, as well as serving as producing clown for several other circuses. Chuck Burnes continues to promote the art of clowning and sees that this special world of entertainment never dies.

MIME

The art of pantomime has been a part of theatre since the early days of the Greco-Roman performers. Without the advantage of today's audio systems, these early performers used masks and pantomime to convey the Story and action of the play. Although the words or dialogue of a play are extremely important it was the action presented through pantomime that kept the interest and attention of the audience.

The entertainers who followed the early Greco-Roman performers continued to refine the art of pantomime. Pantomime was intregal to the performances of the Commedia Dell' Arte, yet is also took on other meanings. Throughout the 18th century popular theatres playing to non-aristocratic audiences were subjected to political harassment. The harassment went as far as denying the right to perform dramatic plays or compelling actors, by law, to remain silent. Actors were now forced to find expression through pantomime.

Pantomime continued to grow and was soon incorporated into the entertainment of the circus. With little time for dialogue and activity occuring all around, the circus clown had to find a way to compete and capture the attention of the audience. Slapstick routines like those of the Commedia Dell' Arte were performed along with pantomime and other physical and sight gags. Clowns, such as Grock, Forto and Grimaldi developed their skills in pantomime to maximize the audience response to their act.

With the rise of music hall entertainment and vaudeville, pantomime again came back to the theatre. Performers, such as Dimitri, Etienne Decroux and Marcel Marceau became the new stars of this art.

The performance styles of today's mimes vary. The master of the 20th century mimes is Marcel Marceau. In the traditional European style, Marcel performs on a stage lit by only a white floodlight, void of any microphone and remaining in total silence. He is known for his extraordinary manipulation of imaginary objects. His movements can make audiences laugh at one moment and bring tears to their eyes in the next. Through his controlled, carefully choreographed movements, he can create almost any scene or object before the eyes of the audience.

Mimes, like Yengibarov and Dimitri have expanded the role of the mime by incorporating the use of real objects. This new hybrid mime is often called "eccentric". With the introduction of motion pictures and later television, the "eccentric" style of pantomime became prominent in the performances of such entertainers as Buster Keaton, Charlie Chaplin, Laurel & Hardy, Red Skelton, Danny Kaye and Jerry Lewis.

Mimes can still be seen and enjoyed today, whether on the stage, in the circus or on a street corner while waiting to see a movie.

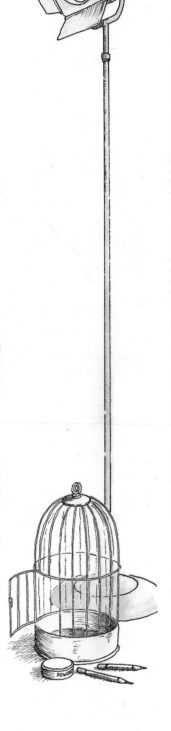

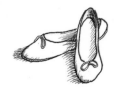

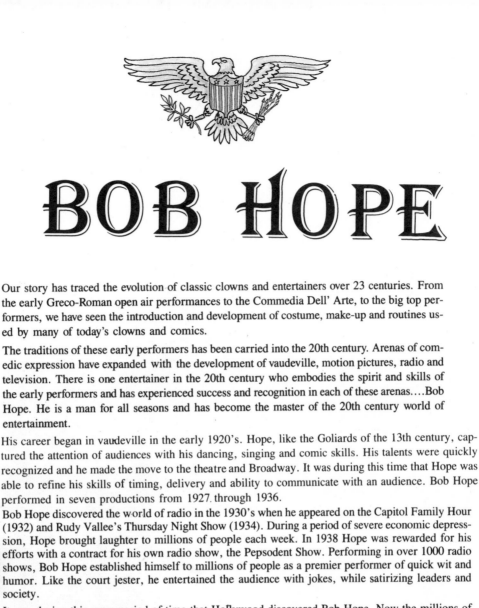

BOB HOPE

Our story has traced the evolution of classic clowns and entertainers over 23 centuries. From the early Greco-Roman open air performances to the Commedia Dell' Arte, to the big top performers, we have seen the introduction and development of costume, make-up and routines used by many of today's clowns and comics.

The traditions of these early performers has been carried into the 20th century. Arenas of comedic expression have expanded with the development of vaudeville, motion pictures, radio and television. There is one entertainer in the 20th century who embodies the spirit and skills of the early performers and has experienced success and recognition in each of these arenas....Bob Hope. He is a man for all seasons and has become the master of the 20th century world of entertainment.

His career began in vaudeville in the early 1920's. Hope, like the Goliards of the 13th century, captured the attention of audiences with his dancing, singing and comic skills. His talents were quickly recognized and he made the move to the theatre and Broadway. It was during this time that Hope was able to refine his skills of timing, delivery and ability to communicate with an audience. Bob Hope performed in seven productions from 1927 through 1936.

Bob Hope discovered the world of radio in the 1930's when he appeared on the Capitol Family Hour (1932) and Rudy Vallee's Thursday Night Show (1934). During a period of severe economic depression, Hope brought laughter to millions of people each week. In 1938 Hope was rewarded for his efforts with a contract for his own radio show, the Pepsodent Show. Performing in over 1000 radio shows, Bob Hope established himself to millions of people as a premier performer of quick wit and humor. Like the court jester, he entertained the audience with jokes, while satirizing leaders and society.

It was during this same period of time that Hollywood discovered Bob Hope. Now the millions of people who had come to know and enjoy Hope on radio, could actually see him. Wasting no opportunity, Bob became involved in movies that featured his verbal humor and his comic physical skills. As always, Bob Hope left the audience laughing in over 70 movies.

Bob Hope has always been concerned with the spirit of his fellow men. In the 1930's, his radio and motion picture comedy got millions of people through the great depression. On May 6, 1941 Bob Hope began a tradition that is unsurpassed in the history of entertainment. He started touring the U.S. military bases around the world, entertaining millions of G.I.'s. In 1948 Hope began his annual Christmas tour which lasted for 22 years. He has brought joy to millions of G.I.'s participating in World War II, Korean War, Vietnam War and other conflicts throughout the world. His few moments on the stage causes the audience to forget their troubles and brings smiles to their faces.

In the 1950's Bob Hope began yet another facet of his career, television. On June 8, 1950 Hope began his long running relationship with N.B.C. television. Appearing in more than 480 shows, Bob Hope has become recognized world wide. The world has shown its appreciation to Bob Hope for his contributions. He has been honored by five American presidents, leaders of many nations, U.S. labor, U.S. Armed Services, U.S.O., U.S. congress, Academy of Arts and Sciences and many other organizations. Hope has over 45 honorary degrees and has had theatres, hospital wards, schools, halls, bridge and most recently, a cultural arts center named in his honor.

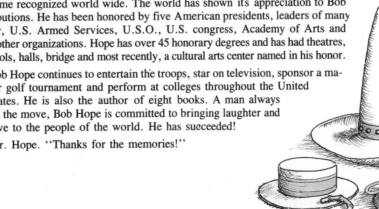

Bob Hope continues to entertain the troops, star on television, sponsor a major golf tournament and perform at colleges throughout the United States. He is also the author of eight books. A man always on the move, Bob Hope is committed to bringing laughter and love to the people of the world. He has succeeded!

Mr. Hope. ''Thanks for the memories!''

Bibliography

Biship, George   *The World of Clowns* 1976 Brooke House Publishers
Northridge California

Clement, Herb, *The Circus - Bigger and Better Than Ever* 1974 A. S. Barnes & Co.
New York, N.Y.

Clowns, Dickens, Charles, *The Memoires of Joseph Grimaldi* 1838 Reprint, 1968
MacGibbon and Lee, London, England

Cohen, Gustave, *LaGrande Clarte du Moyen-Age* 1967 Gallimard, Paris, France

Dictionnaire, *des Oeuvres de tous les temps et de tous les pays* 1952-54,
Laffont Bompiani, Paris, France

Disher, Maurice Willson, *Clowns & Pantomimes* 1968 M. Willson Disher & B. Blom
New York, N.Y.

Ducharte, Pierre-douis, *The Italian Comedy* 1966 Dover Books, New York, N.Y.

Fenner, Mildred and Wolcott, *The Circus — Lure and Legend* 1970 Prentice Hall
New York, N.Y.

Hugill, Benyl, *Bring on the Clowns* 1980 Chartweell Books, Sea Cau Cus

Rowse, A. L., ed., *The Annotated Shakespeare* 1984, Longmeadow Press
New York, N.Y.

Smith, Winifred, *The Commedia Dell' Arte* 1964 Blom Publications New York, N.Y.

Spaight, George *The Book of Clowns* 1980 MacMillan Publishers New York, N.Y.

Swartzell, Lowell, *Here Come the Clowns* 1978 Viking Press New York, N. Y.

Willeford, William, *The Fool and His Sceptor* 1969 Northwestern University Press
Evanston, Illinois

Hope, Bob, *The Last Christmas Show*, 1974 Doubleday, New York, N.Y.